I0132393

penchant

penchant

AMANDA J. COBB

PENCHANT

Design and cover art by:
Studio Guerassio
www.studioguerassio.com

ISBN-13: 978-0-6151-4841-0

Third Edition: July 2016

ISBN 978-0-615-14841-0

90000

9 780615 148410

TABLE OF *contents*

observations

introspections

leavetakings

quirks

notes

about the author

acknowledgements

with love to:

| My Mom & Sisters

some of the strongest women I know,
for rubbing off on me;

| My Dad

who I think would've been proud
and wish he could've seen this;

and

| Ian

my better half, for unwavering love
and support in everything I do.

observations

BREATHE, & I'LL *drift away*

I am teetering,
poised on the edge of a sharp blade of grass
between clouds and concrete -
rife with tension and calm,
a breath away from flight or fall.

        I have achieved
        perfect, dangerous balance.

And you,
hurtling on a course
set to slam into me,
don't have the courtesy
to let me first discover

        if my wings are made of wax or lead.

SKYSCRAPERS
& THE CRANES THAT BUILD THEM

I've seen the world's skylines
where they meet the clouds -
New York, Paris, Sydney...
countless lofty others.

Each has a distinct shape and feel,
their own sharp edge against the twilight.

Yet always, I feel choked,
trapped,
caged in by walls and towers
built so close
and so high
I lose myself
and the horizon.

What use in building towards the sky
when you can no longer see it?

These monstrosities of steel and glass
are cited by some
as the pinnacles of human achievement.
I can understand;
we are so small
compared to what we create.

But what, then, does that make of our gods?

hardcore

I watched you run
in circles at the concert,
dizzying yourself up in time
to your daddy's music.
Around and around
ran your little feet,
clad in miniature white sneakers,
until a stray stranger's foot
caught the tip of yours
and you went crashing down
to the rugged pavement -
knee, then elbow, then head.

      If humans left skidmarks,
      you would have.

And yet, there was no crying,
no trembling of lip
or doctoring of hurts.
You were simply stunned a moment,
then pushed your 18-month-old self up,
giving your worried and frazzled mom
a huge grin,
and began again to run in circles,
face lit up happily and arms,
if scraped, still in the air.

RETREATING
force

You doubt my omnipotence,
my existence, vast and timeless;
sadly, I can understand.

If I see and know all,
if I create and control all,
why do such atrocities
still happen in this garden?

My children, your ignorance grieves me.

I gave over control
of the greater part of your destinies
the very moment you became
beings independent of me.

Free will has been both bane and blessing.

You are free to make
your own choices, yes;
once in a century or so, you
prove yourselves capable of such genius,
but then always fall back
to squabbling over irrelevancies.

And I cannot interfere. That
was the limitation I put
on my own power
the day you were born.

I try, I do try
to reach you,
to make you once again
remember what is truly important,
what is sacred,
how you should live -

does not the sun still rise
on spring mornings to sparkle
on leaf-caught dewdrops?

Doesn't the ocean still pound on the shore
in my age-old pattern?

Is there not still love and beauty,
birth and death, wonder
and salvation?

The living world I gave to you
is a sacrament, as are you,
though you have forgotten,

just as you have forgotten that
you possess the gift of free thought
and what that implies about blame.

As if Heaven forbid you take
responsibility for your own lives.

I assure you, it's quite the opposite.

THE
hillside

The hillside was covered
with polymer marble relics
strewn over the crisp spring grass -
manufactured in our modern age
and abandoned to look the dubious part
of the broken and crumbling classicism
that is supposed to lend us some prestige.

It did give that bit of hillside
a play of lights and shadows
that followed the arcing sun
across the carpeted lawn and clover.

I looked on from my shaded alcove
among the roots of the willow tree,
noting the irony in an entire race
lying on its resume.

WATER _falls_

Newton caught an apple on the head
and thought he had discovered
the basic principle
that governs the world of men -
why rain falls
and rivers tumble down cliffsides,
why arrows shot up come down
and pigs can't fly.

    But that's just physics;
    falling tears are never blamed on gravity.

GAS STATION
insights #12

He comes inside,
in ragged, too-baggy jeans,
one ear filled with metal
and his arms with violent tattoos.
He saunters up,
investigating the pop cooler -
a comment about only drinking juice
barely audible above the traffic noise outside.
Unsatisfied, he turns to
the candy racks.
A few minutes,
and he shakes his head.
A mutter:
"No, better not.
That shit'll rot your teeth."
He grins at me -
one tooth missing.

Then he steps outside
and lights a cigarette.

history HISTORY

White man's history
is a school bully
who can only feel good
when putting others down.

compline

Night has fallen again, infinite
dark eternally regular.
And why shouldn't it be?
Why should I presume on you to notice
such trivialities - a simple broken heart,
one small death - in this immensity?

There is a field beside my house,
full of dandelions and clover
and knee-high, yellowed grass -
small jet ants and racestriped chipmunks
expire there as regular as a sundial's shadow
weathering the face of stone hours.

Do I deign to wear black for them?

You don your raven cloak
each evening, it's true;
but I don't believe for a moment
that any of this dim panoply is for me.
This was your routine
long before my trifling grief,

and even before yours.

THE *helium balloon's* THREAT

It drifts quietly through the house
in the aftermath of the party,
suspended at neck level
by the unseen and halfhearted
currents of stale air.

It seems a lonely, aimless thing,
half-dead already -
a depressingly elastic red
against the grey
of returned normalcy.

How brief excitement,
cheer,
its use
lasts.

No longer new enough to burst,
it is capable only
of fading,
forgotten until found once again,
wrinkled and underfoot.

where i want to be

This is pure nature -
wild, raw, unadorned.

Beautiful and abundant to those
who are willing to learn, to see;
harshly unforgiving to those who trespass.

This is primal testing ground,
at once ancient and fresh.

There are no subway maps here,
no gruff gas station attendants
to give directions.
No *convenience* stores or fast food.
No locks or feather pillows or hot water.

Out here, the civilized world means nothing.
Out here, mistakes can get you killed.

And so help me, I find that incredibly
refreshing.

This is life whittled down
to the true necesseties.
This is life with challenge,
life requiring skill.

In a world that revolves around
safety and sanitation and political correctness,
this is a reality with meaning.

SONNET #/

How cruelly the Fates do spin their plan
upon the loom of wretched lives and great,
ensnaring both the wise and careless man
with threads that end each one at Hades' gate.
No dream or hope survives that fatal weave -
the golden shears, a-flashing, cut them all
and as the shades from former bodies leave,
the wants and wishes, into darkness, fall.
The loved ones whom, in life, get left behind
are Fated to existence full of grief
and marks man thought would stand for all of time
are in malicious jest but very brief.

       And yet we strive each day our souls to sing,
       forgetful of the Fates' unkindly string.

introspections

IN SOUND

a self portrait

I am a symphony,
a harmonic cacophony -

the sound of laughter
of pages rustling, turning
of a camera shutter
of typing keys

the sound of a pen whirring over the lines
a piano concerto
an audience's applause
a curtain falling

the sound of a tear slipping down a cheek
of the muscles stretching into a smile

the sound of the ocean

the sound of the wind

the sound of flight

the sound of miles passing as the tires turn
a door opening
chocolates unwrapped
a cat purring

the sound of differences accepted
of things unspoken
my sisters' joys
my mother's sighs -

I am every note.

ideally...

A warm beach
and salty waves.

Sunshine.

Paid to travel with my camera,
capturing art.
Paid to put my soul into words.

A sense of adventure
in everyday life.

A family.

Love, happiness, satisfaction.

Minimal regrets.

A feisty old age.

mother/lust

A little girl sits next to me on the boat
and says I have pretty hair.

I see my lover's clear eyes
in her freckled, dimpled face.

But she isn't mine.

My womb aches for a moment
at its monthly cycle of sterile pills.

My mind consoles:
but there's still so much to do.

BELOW THE surface

She sits in the corner,
a soft gradient of golden-brown tints
in the filtered morning sunlight.

Named as beautiful these days,
by familiars and strangers alike,
(and for once they mean
below the surface, too)
she still remembers days
lived with shame in wire-rims and braces
and creative names thrown at her
by boys with perfect teeth
and girls with eyeliner eyes.

She smiles at how little it matters,
now that she's come into her own,
finding her confidence
and proving what she's really worth.

Yet each time she finds herself
walking through a crowd alone,
head bowed,
her eyes spark with anger
at how deep they managed to cut.

Memories are sometimes easier to leave behind
than habits born for years.

GAS STATION INsights #15

She stands behind the counter in the noontime heat,
hair up in an untidy knot that tells the world
she doesn't really mind what her hair looks like
as long as it stays off her neck.
Wearing whatever clothes she happened to grab
in the predawn dark,
she drums her fingers on the countertop,
silver, serpentine jewelry flashing in the sun
and hums along as she sorts out
the melody her latest song will follow.
Her eyes move to the clock counting down
to the end of her shift
and impatience pulls her into a restless pacing
and she watches her feet as they move
across the worn tiles.
Her toenails are silver, too, dirty around the edges
from walking around the autoshop
barefoot but for her beaded sandals.
She examines her fingernails, ever an uneven mess,
and she doesn't really care that they are uneven,
but it gives her something to do.
When someone walks in she looks up from her seat
through black lashes made to stand out
by the only makeup she ever wears
and takes their money
and gives the correct change
in a simple, efficient, polite transaction
that allows her to go back to
drumming and humming, pacing and examining
while she waits for the clock
to count down two more hours.

fingernail
CLIPPINGS

A metallic clip, snip, release
and the fingernail clippings fall
one by one, bit by bit,
in a sporadic rhythm, downward spiral,
to land with a soft rustle
against the plastic of the garbage bag.

Falling through the air softly,
like snowflakes,
but they are just dead cells -
expendable,
disposable.

A wicked grin.

Besides, he said he was tired
of the red trails down his back.

WATCH YOUR
heartstrings

The crag says to the pebble,
Careful of those you love -
they rip away at any moment.

Well, Death has always kept pace at my elbow.

Shrewd queen of foresight,
I carry my own scythe.

apologia ——————————

No, everything's not alright.

But you already knew that.
Everyone knows that;
it's the universal truth.

If everything was fine,
no one would need to ask.

I don't want you to, either.
Asking just adds to it;
it's nothing you can fix,
and I can't articulate it anyway.

And no, it isn't going to be alright.
It doesn't just disappear.

It's always there, in some degree,
intense or subtle,
screaming or melting.

It doesn't go away,
no matter how much you
or I
wish it would.

And I don't tell you this for sympathy
or pity
or because I want some solution;
there isn't one.

I tell you because sometimes being alone
is the best way to cope,
and sometimes it's not.

But if you could be there
to offer silent comfort
and just a touch of understanding...

it might make it a bit easier.

leavetakings

RAINBOWS
Ryan adams &
_____

I saw a rainbow over the highway today,
as I drove away from where I left my heart
and I could feel the tug of those strings
strung along the red ridge of those colors,
arching back to you,
like my thoughts as I listen to Ryan Adams
singing that love doesn't play games anymore
and the words are beautiful,
but they don't touch me here
because I can't agree to that.

I drive into the evening,
into the setting sun
watching the sky swallow that one rainbow
and be embodied by color
covering the atmosphere from horizon to horizon -
wisps of clouds as jewelry,
the sun a crown of molten gold -
and I appreciate the irony
of driving west into a ball of fire
when I left my only light back in the east.

I turn the engine off as my road comes to an end,
just as the sun sinks beyond the rim of earth,
plunging me into the darkness alone
and I realize how empty darkness can be
when I have no heart or light to fight it,
having left the stars with you,
like so much else,
and I thought of Ryan Adams again,
agreeing with a meaning he didn't intend,
for this is certainly not a game.

I fall apart ~~as you~~ fall asleep

Worn out and stretched thin
from endless nights
spent watching subtitled movies
from countries I've never seen
because I couldn't sleep
with this heart full of unasked questions
since I reminded you that
I'll be boarding a plane
for the other side of the world soon,
and you laid complacent next to me,
only saying that it will be
interesting.

to mikey

On His 21st Birthday

I learned of your death today,

a chance encounter in my email,
mixed in between the horoscopes and headlines
with the unobtrusive and understated subject
'Sad News.'

It was warm and raining outside,
exactly the opposite of how I felt.

I couldn't really grasp it, even as
I stared blankly at pictures of you in my albums;
in each one you are wearing a huge smile,
your trademark.
A part of me knew I'd never see that smile again,
but still I couldn't cry.

Hours later,
on a bus traveling under clear and colored skies,
I looked up and saw the clouds
painted in the setting sun's palette,
and it was so vast
and beautiful
and eternal.

I thought of you again, gone,
but out there somewhere
in all of that beauty
and finally I began to cry.

I HAVE
SCARS

One through the palm
from that cross you nailed me to
on the muddy field,
in your mind,
forever thinking I should sacrifice myself
for you.

One through the heart
as you made me choose,
unfairly,
between love and freedom,
when I should have found them
in each other.

parting _Is In No Way sweet_

I'm missing a star
from my sky - the warmth
that watched over my sleep,
the light I plucked from
all the rest to give to you,
to bring you back, arcing,
blazing. The night has sunk
to darkest black, and I want
it back. I want you here.

The seeing don't cherish light
until it's gone; forgive me,
I was blind. I thought I had
long ago learned what lessons
love and pain could teach.

When two becomes habit,
preference and comfort,
one is so much harder. Air waves
can't compete with the night sky
and your eyes. Extra space
doesn't make things less crowded,
like they say - just lonelier.

And I, who never cry, fed my pillow
salt all afternoon, in the dark,
in the silence. And where that
point of light should have been
was a hole, a lack that screamed
your absence. And I felt it,
walked right up to the edge
of nothing and looked - a reflection;
my drained face, a night with no
stars, black and bitter.

i stuck a pen in my heart TO WRITE THIS

I broke down today

right in the middle of playing
a goddamned piano song,
that one from Evita
that you always liked

and all I could think of
were all of the things
you never heard me play
or saw me create
or watched me accomplish
and I know such things would've made you
happy, maybe even proud

and I can't help wondering
why you didn't think that
was worth staying around for.

God, even now, years later,
you still can make me
break down, sobbing,
at the smallest reminder.

I know the best way
to get over what you did
is to turn my sorrow to anger,
blame you for it, completely,
as is perhaps fair -

I could disdain you for being a coward,
for choosing the easy way out.

Damn it, I wanted you to see all of this!
I needed you to be a part
of this life that you created.
I wanted you there when I first went to college,
and when I graduated.
I still want you back
to walk me down the aisle,
to hold your grandchildren,
to be a part of so many things.
And I could easily come
to hate you
for robbing each of these moments from me

But the truth is
I miss you too much.
You were a good father,
and I loved you,
and it seems I have to choose
between pain over how you left me
or tainting sixteen years of memories with hate.

Either way, I've still lost you.
I'm crying as I write this,
and I know it won't be the last time.

REQUIEM
in the whitecaps

I was angry,
angry at the fact
that the last image I would ever have of you
would be of your ashes
poured out of a cheap, plastic bag,
the one before it no better -
you, motionless,
streaks down your cheeks and on the wall
and cold, so cold,
as the lake you are now a part of forever
with the north wind
turning my tears to paths of ice.

And yes, I cried;
Of course I cried -
I ran from my dry family
to sit solitary on sand-scoured driftwood,
the kind of place I would have found you, once
and a spider crawled along it
towards me; I just looked at it -
you had always dealt with my spiders,
my monsters,
but you were gone.
You are gone.

I looked out onto the lake,
the lake turned your eternal grave
your frozen tomb,
ringed by the beach of tide-washed rocks
we used to gather together,
and every wave echoed my grief,
their soft roaring sussurations
crying out Why, Why, Why
as they washed on the rocks
and then they flowed back out,
taking my anger with them,
and all that was left
among the cold and the pain
was a faint and fading I Love You.

quirks

the world is all blurry
WITHOUT MY
G L A S S E S

You took my clarity
and ran,
daring me to follow you
through minefields
and six-lane traffic,
never imagining for a minute
that I would make it.

I have depth perception
of space,
not people.

And I don't wear my contacts
because my pain is your prerogative,
and I wouldn't want to see
the look of glee on your face anyway.

COMPULSIVE liar

I am not sarcastic.

I am everything I ever wanted to be.
I believe in my power to change things.

I have no regrets.
I am never disappointed with myself.
I never cry.

I get enough sleep.
I don't ever eat junk food.
I exercise regularly.
I never bite my nails or crack my knuckles.

I do not procrastinate.
I never wear the same shirt twice without washing it.
I don't speed on the highway.
I am extremely organized.
I never give up.

I understand myself completely.
I only keep my good memories.
I know what I want from life.
I don't fear anything.
I am not alone.
I am happy.

I never lie.

THE
dancers

Trapped in the dark,
waiting, wondering,
not in silence, but worse - a neverending buzz
that drowns the unhearing ears

Able to dance like nobody's watching
because nobody is
Alone in the blackness, blundering
and stumbling into others equally alone

And then the world turns over
and sharp bursts of riotous sunlight invade

The dancers pause, dazzled and confused,
and then all is chaos, a frenzy
No longer alone,
but overwhelmed
Too many, too much, too quickly
The light hurts, but it calls
and the darkness,
stable and familiar,
is gone

An upward rush towards the blazing drum
that every wing beats to
in the light and the motion
of the frantic dancers
that seem merely flitting shadows,
ethereal and transient souls
caught up in the whirlwind
of sudden, inconceivable freedom.

mariposa

Mi madre, the widow, she grows
butterfly bushes in front
of our dead-end house, to start
a collection, colored shapes
of wings and eyes to put
behind glass, hang
on the wall - sadism
made beautiful. Twenty years
those bushes have grown
and though they come,
the mariposas, fluttering lives,
she has yet to find
los caídos to perpetuate
her hobby. Her shelves are full
of dust and ghosts. But then
where should we go
to recover the wisps
of dreams long dead?
I stare at the wings
pinned to my wall,
a Mardi Gras mask, a butterfly
in dark and wilted feathers,
the mimicry no more
alive than the original,
like the pipevine caught
and Christed in a display case.
The feathers stir in stale
air currents, remembered
flight - the bird, their former
home, as much a fiction now
as the enigmatic figure such
green-black tufts used to
personify, as the person
I once thought I knew
myself to be. Age
has turned daring matador;
the muleta is gone and
I am face-to-face
with its pins.

el Vuelo

I close my eyes
and can hear the ground rumbling -
thunder or earthquake, a Mack truck
or just the aire acondicionado
blowing lukewarm, I don't know.
The air smelled of brown sugar
on Thursday - azúcar marrón.
Marrón, el mar, the sea - my older sister
by the sea in México, brown as the sun
will make her, browner than any non-Latino
should be, as the needle plunges into her back
copying her art, eyes stylized
like a mask of feathers, eyes closed.
A thousand miles away, just as brown,
the sea of her name in her eyes,
Marisa, the little one, cannot sleep.
Eyes open, open and waiting -
full of salt and hope of salvation
long-delayed. She doesn't sit in churches,
but goes also to the sea, ever
preferring salt to sugar, wounds still
open. Still she does not sleep.
I, too, visit the sea, but I don't live there.
I am white like the salt
and pale like the sand, in shades
of gold, oro. With open eyes
I look up. I see - clouds, blue,
the golden sun, el sol de oro,
my soul, the wind, el aire libre -
libertad, freedom. I close my eyes
and dream of flight.

LEAVING *limbo*

Sometimes
leaving Limbo
simply means that
things get
worse.

even among ascetics

Lack of comparison
becomes lack of definition,
uncertain existence -
ethereal, ephemeral fiction.

Those with a stomach for truth
are bound to go hungry.

science fiction & FANTASY

Alongside one another on
the shelves, as if the two
have more in common than the space
they share. It used to be

that elves stuck to their forests and
the aliens to their moons.
Old Robin Hood was safe from napalm
and Yoda could avoid

the insecurities of height
when next to Merlin. But
the nearness of bookstore shelves
has bent the line between -

now sorcerers carry M-16s
and dragons fly the stars
on ships. The genres have been blurred,
the categories tossed.

Industrialization has
invaded fancy's world,
impossibility crept in
on reason. And what for?

Convenience in stocking? The
efficiency of bulk
identity? Well, give me back
the knights with swords, the elves

with bow and arrows. Refuse
Han's bid on Chimaera,
keep Predator out of the ball.
Draw back that line in bold.

Put science fiction and fantasy
on separate shelves again -
fun worlds within themselves, but really,
some things should never mix.

shadows & ANGELS

The same age-old feud
of light versus dark
commences once again.
The battlefield is a blur,
half shadows,
half angels,
and it's hard to tell
the light from the fire
and the dark from the starry sky.
Dark claws greedily at the soul
while light desperately defends...

or is it the other way around?

INJUSTICES on the
of dirty dishes

Thrown casually aside into a pile,
indifferently stacked and pressed up against strangers,
like a body count of war victims
dumped all into an unmarked grave.

Discarded as soiled, impure,
bacterial shame colors their faces
in the wake of their hygienic rape.

Forcefully tortured with 3rd-degree aquatic burns
only to have bristle-and-wire pads scraped across them,
their skin rubbed raw for faultless blemishes,
uncommitted crimes -
innocents punished for the flaws of their masters.

Parts of themselves carved away,
or smoothed over,
the psychologist of the sink
replacing them all into carbon-copy rows,
identical, cleansed faces normal once more.

opossums

He says,
Opossums!
Opossums, it is,
big, hairy opossums
have lodged in my lungs,
choking my breath,
and in their death throes
are clawing my insides to shreds!

Opossums? I ask.

Well, yes, says he.
I would have said dingoes,
but they are not native to this area.

WHERE did THE god OF THE PURITANS go?

The archangels had another spat
over why Peter should be the only one
to have the fun of being bouncer
at the gates of the Oyster Club,
while they were stuck with menial jobs
like 'messenger' and 'guardian'.
So they formed a workers union
and went to God's office to complain.

God wasn't at work, though.
He'd simply left, and taped
a hastily-scrawled note to his door
that said:

Buddha had another narcoleptic fit,
Allah stubbed his toe,
and Ishtar is on vacation with her latest lover,
so Mars, Equus, Hera, and Thor
needed another player for
the Intertheological Kickball Finals.

Be back in an eon or two.

notes

"Breathe, & I'll Drift Away" was written in response to a topic given by PPS member Lindsay Sanders.

"Hardcore" is dedicated to the youngest child of the lead singer of the band Anonymous Bosch.

"Retreating Force" and "Compline" are imitations of poet Louise Glück.

"The Hillside," "Skyscrapers & the Cranes that Build Them," "The Helium Balloon's Threat," "Fingernail Clippings," "Requiem in the Whitecaps," and "Even Among Ascetics" were all written in response to topics given from PPS member Joe Chiles.

"Water Falls" and "On the Injustices of Dirty Dishes" were written in response to topics given by my sister, also a PPS member, Katrina Cobb. "Water Falls" was also the poem with which I won the Stephen M. Schwartz Prize in Poetry from Marietta College.

"Where I Want to Be" is about Australia, where I studied abroad for a semester.

"Sonnet #1" is an attempt at a Shakespearean sonnet.

"To Mikey, on his 21st Birthday" is dedicated to Michael Joseph Conte, 11-28-1983 to 11-28-2004.

"The World is All Blurry Without My Glasses" was inspired by my longtime college roommate Kate Paullin uttering the title sentence at 3:30 a.m.

"The Dancers" was inspired by an article telling of a truckload of beehives that overturned on the highway.

"Mariposa" is an attempt at an imitation of poet Rane Arroyo, as is "El Vuelo." Apologies for not explaining all of the Spanish terms, but you can look them up yourself if they weren't clear.

"Science Fiction & Fantasy" is an imitation of poet Andrew Hudgins. And, just for the record, I love to read sci-fi/fantasy and have no objections when they mix.

"Opossums" is a direct transcription of an actual conversation with one of my best friends, Josh A. Green.

"Where Did the God of the Puritans Go?" was inspired by my U.S. Literature professor, Dr. Carol Steinhagen, asking the question in the title.

Both Gas Station Insights were inspired during my time working as a gas station cashier for a few years in high school.

works previously published

Pulse, Marietta College, 2004
    "Where Did the God of The Puritans Go?"
    "Breathe, & I'll Drift Away"
    "On the Injustices of Dirty Dishes"

Confluence, Ohio Valley Literary Group, Vol.16
    "Compulsive Liar"

about the author

Amanda J. Cobb

graduated in 2006 from Marietta College in Ohio with
a BFA in Graphic Design. Her poems were published in
Marietta College's *Pulse* and also in a regional collection
called *Confluence*. This is her first solo book. She is a
long-time member of the online Pathetic Poets Society
(www.pathetic.org).

She is now married and runs her own business (Studio
Guerassio) as a graphic designer in Austin, Texas, where
she lives with her husband and dog.

Though her main creative outlets are screenprinting
and photography, she has long admitted to a decided
penchant for poetry.

Personal blog: www.dragonflightdreams.com
Design studio: www.studioguerassio.com

acknowledgements

Thanks, first and always, to my family, for their continued and unwavering (if sometimes confused) support. Thanks to fellow members of the Pathetic Poets Society (www.pathetic.org) Katrina Cobb, Joe Chiles, and Paul Lastovica for their long-term poetic inspiration and advice, and for help with the selection of pieces for this book. Thanks to Kate Paullin, Ashley Vincelli and Scott Nyitray for letting me gripe to them whenever the stress got to me during the development of the first edition of this book. Thanks to Josh A. Green, Andrew Schuch, and Derek Law for their continuing optimism and faith in my talent. Thanks also to Sam Armacost and again to Kate Paullin for discovering Lulu.com, which made it much easier for me republish this edition of the book. And thanks to my husband, Ian, for everything.

www.ingramcontent.com/pod-product-compliance
Lightning Source LLC
Chambersburg PA
CBHW031332040426
42443CB00005B/304